VALLEY
SUTRA

1 2 3 4 5 6 – 14 13 12 11 10 09

Caitlin Press Inc.
8100 Alderwood Road,
Halfmoon Bay, BC V0N 1Y1
www.caitlin-press.com

Edited by Kate Braid and Marisa Alps.
Text design by Vici Johnstone.
Cover design by Michelle Winegar.
Printed in Canada.

Caitlin Press Inc. acknowledges financial support from the Government of Canada
through the Book Publishing Industry Development Program and the Canada Council
for the Arts, and from the Province of British Columbia through the British Columbia
Arts Council and the Book Publisher's Tax Credit.

Library and Archives Canada Cataloguing in Publication

Gill, Kuldip, 1934–
    Valley sutra / Kuldip Gill.
Poems.
ISBN 978-1-894759-36-6
    I. Title.
PS8563.I47976V35 2009   C811'.54   C2009-905591-0

VALLEY
SUTRA

KULDIP GILL

CAITLIN PRESS

Table of Contents

The Mill Town

Bill Miner's Notebook

The Mill Town

Alpha Towns — The Valley's North Shore

Sporadically along the North Shore they stand
alpha women faces to the south, gaze down
scan the valleys, the lay of the land,
arms crossed against the east wind
backs to the north, their hair
brushing red, gold, brown and black against
rows of indigo blue mountains.

But there is one and I know her, away
from the rest she stands legs apart, feet
planted firm along the track, above
the line of the river, her arms crossed
high overhead, waiting above the
CPR station, the water tower, hotel and Legion.
Climb the contours up and up, touch
stars, the tracking satellites, see for yourself
her hills, ravines, midnight concupiscent mountains.

She does not give herself easily. There
are mounds and stairs, hills and winding
streams, waterfalls. Bells chime over her, peeling
each single two-note toll, they ring
this-one, this-one, this-one, here,
this-one, this-one, this-one, here.

The Mills of Mission — Embers and Sparks

Townspeople ran down the hills
awakened as the river glowed,
the sky fountained ember and spark
and the sirens called their night alarms,
and we got up from our beds,
and held onto a mother's hands.
See the red against black river water—
embers tongue the sky.
Smoke fountains red, grey, black glints and sparkles
that zing and sputter against
streams of water. We stood side by side
and watched men with hands deep in their pockets,
arms crossed high on their chests, watch
the mill burn. Friends stood shoulder to shoulder (and
who knows who is an enemy) in this burning black night.

Steamy wet ash smolders at the edges
of half-burnt, smoking cedar, wet hemlock, fir,
its pitch sputtering and popping.

The smell and sound of a mill on fire.

We ran down the hills and down Horne
to the flats to stand with our kin
their faces glowing red
in the night, grey, by day. We ran.
We ran as children, and then again as adolescents
and as adults, and even now as the mill burns into our old age.

Letter to Peter Trower—Sechelt Peninsula, BC

Dear Peter:
You were only half-right in your poem
"The mill was our mother."
If we didn't attend her there was her other side, remember?
She turned into a hag. Uncontrollable.
You were right when you called her erratic.
One of her other avatars, incarnations
was dark. Kali-like, she could be
a creator or destroyer. And lately, Peter,
that bitch was no mother.

Her vahana is fire
white hot sparks and embers.
She rides them, crackling and angry.
Peter, you forgot that.
Or is it that you saw her only
as a creator?
She was schizophrenic. Kali, a destroyer.

She chewed off arms, legs and
rolled the men around her
gnashed her steel teeth,
spewed out ground
that burned, smoked and smoldered
all night long.

She was mother, and nourished us
but needed constant propitiation to keep her

from her burns and rages, from devouring
the town. We tried, Peter, because
the mill was our mother.

Sometimes, before our eyes
she burned herself—Sati-like—
to the ground. Peter,
she did it again last night and now
she dances on the embers wearing human
skulls of her children rattling around her neck.
That hag was no mother last night, Peter.
She was Kali.

Mill Yard Sounds

That bricolage of mill sounds,
a screech of each saw-cut as the head sawyer pulled down,
the rolling gears of the log-haul,
the whistle to shut down as men moved lumber
down the greenchain, and everything dripped water.
The hemlock, fir, cedar sawdust rose cumulus and turbaned
around heads of mill-men, the forklift driving in and backing out
its burden locked in its arms, and the horns of the honking truck—
a driver impatient for the load of lumber. The chainbelt
clanging as it conveyed clumped wood and bark into
the burner, smoke and embers fssting and spitting.
They sat on the lumber with tin lunch buckets
open, eating curries, achars and rotis in the sun.

The Mill Where the Men Worked (1920s)

Youbou. I dig among the stone
steps and paths you walked.
Breathe the same tepid air
switched by cedar and look to see
what you saw in this land,
its mountains, rocks, fog,
the unending sea's cold water,
reflected sky.

I want to know where you sat
after you pulled green lumber all day.
The mill across the bay, the smell
of sawdust, and pitch from cedar, fir, hemlock
and spruce mingled with sweat in your clothes.

I'm here. Are you a shape in the trees,
hovering omnipotence or watching spirit,
a tenth insight group?

I want a sign from you.
Would you have chosen this spot?
Does an aesthetic run in the blood?

Rain and mist, yet
the sun beams through cloud onto a flat jade rock.
It says: *here I am, your table.*

The picnic hamper in my hands,
full: grapes, mango, cheddar
and brie cheeses, bread.

The green stone's striations
undulate, a pointed head writhes
flickers its red lightening tongue:
Not here! Not here! And
slithers away.

Their sign: *Be watchful
of green granite stones,
the long grasses.*

Here be snakes.

Mill Kids — After School

Children ambled to play amidst
piles of two-by-fours, three-by-sixes, four-by-sixes
end-coloured, end-stamped, tallied to three decimal points
with legal papers (in triplet) for market in Britain and Japan

bounced on lumber ends, ones with the oddest lengths
bounced so that they slapped and tottered
bounced until they toppled, toppled, toppled

ran from the yard to wander down
to the box factory where the owner's daughter Mabel sat
stapling boxes for berry farms, for canneries,
collected throw-away balsam
strips to make airplanes, shaped boats they
reefed from the wharf into the river below
where old Indian women with pails
scooped up silver oolichans by the hundreds as they
edged into the sand banks to lay, alay, alay

ambled home in time to watch
uncles pick slivers from their hands with
sewing needles, their palms dotted with blood
splashed with hydrogen peroxide its fuzz
and fizzle and begged to have some drizzled on a palm
where it sat—a drop without any fizzle or zing, zing

ate their meal, quarrelling and swatting each other

carried wood to heat the house, wet
hemlock stacked to dry, its bark steaming beside the barrel stove,
scratched at the wet sawdust and the slivered welts on their arms
and day at its end, went to bed
to dream, to dream aday, aday

ambled across the tracks in the morning, uphill, all those stairs
and into class again. Everyday.

The Clicks and Snaps of a School Day

Our teacher could smell bras.
Or perhaps it was breasts.
Two of us had them in grade six.
He knew. During assignment time
everyone heads down and working
he paced the room and as he came to me,
boldly snapped the baby blue silk elastic
on my back. Then did the same
to V. I hated him back.

The ruler was near at hand.
Often as he walked by
he clicked the boys behind the ears
or flicked them hard with his fingernails.

He walked from desk to blackboard and back
around the room with a four-inch piece
of chalk. With twenty-five years of experience, his thumbnail
sheared off bits that flew at us
like pea-shooter peas. The floor was spotted white.

History, as history. We got to "Indja," finally
and I learned that in Calcutta
there was a black hole into which all of us Indians threw
all his good white friends. Everyone looked at me
and I remembered nothing. Not a thing about it.
But my guilt was written all over my face. I was twelve.
The click of a black hole in Calcutta had come full turn to me.

Mission's Pied Piper (1945)

From dull school classes
suddenly, kids heard the clang and a low mooing sound.
There was no dismissal, everyone dashed downstairs
down the hill, through the town, hundreds of kids running
down the middle of the road
down to the river,
down to the wharf
heeding the piper's call,
the sternwheeler,
Oh! Joy!
The *Samson*
was back
in town!

The Gulley

The playground path beside the school, the ravine.
Vine maple and brush knowing the fuzz of triple-bud hazelnuts.
Down the gulley straight down go their winged feet
their voices along its walls echoed, run!
don't stop, don't stop, you'll fall, you'll fall! Run
through leaf-loam of branches, needles, leaves, waiting
fecund and fetid with moisture and rain, black, soft under
the light-footed child going down sideways cutting
a horizontal path along the vertical drop of the gulley.
Fast, holding fast to the magenta flower, brush and grass
and infant tip of a branch coming off in a hand
surprised by the odd scotch thistle its prick and needle yet going
sideways, down and around and further and
further down to stop
by the creek edge.
The fern around it luminous,
waxy tips of things just below the mulchen bed,
waiting to unfurl silken in the spring
and upright with heads yet curled.
Until her feet slid into them, to stop.

The Stream at the Bottom of the Gulley

What is left of the thin water strands when they reach the sea?
Once, a silken ice-cold thread flowed down the gulley
gurgled, roiled self-absorbed in its furl through
to the river cutting Second Street, Main Street,
the flats, and around the hobo jungle in its rush to join
the mud-grey river to sea.

It is a liminal creek now
stopped by a steel gate that regulates its flow.
Where once, dammed, it was the town's swimming hole,
now it's under blacktop, a parking lot on Second Street
under the town of Mission on Main
and the industrial sites fill the flats,
below. Does it reach the river, now?

Seventeen — Summer Job at Aylmer's Cannery

I got the call: *Be on the morning shift at seven* AM.
At the conveyor belt we picked and snapped green beans
molded them, long and hot, into tins, picked up the tins
four at a time with claw-like hands and put them
on the salt water lines, the smell a cross between steamed
clams and cod-liver oil. The belt spat
infant green-white seeds, and innards, worms,
and long bean strings.

The fun shift was the sugar shift in the attic where we lolled
over sugar bags stacked by hundreds, talking,
laughing, sometimes flirting, our job indolent, slow-going until
they banged on the pipes
from the first floor, the signal for
more sugar! More!
Then we jumped, grabbed knives, cut bags, poured sugar
into hoppers, over the top and down
into our clothes, hair and shoes, sticky sweet
in the sweat and heat.

We were a team, but Rob
didn't know a thing, and when the four-inch belt
flipped off the ceiling pulley, he flapped both hands and
shouted at me to do something!
I grab and squeeze the loop in the middle, lift it up
over the upper pulley, deftly roll
my hand outside and over the lower pulley. Done.

Roger called him a sissy, (though we girls knew
he had an effeminate gentle muse). He let a girl
do the dangerous work that could tear off a hand.
Our team called me, *Sam, Sam the fixit ma'am.*

On the berry line someone brought stacked crates
stuffed tins for me to move with my claw-like hands,
four at a time onto a conveyor belt that
moved them under nozzles shooting
syrup from the tank above. Hot syrup
foamed and splashed all over me.
Three AM I punched the timecard out,
my hands and body crisp,
glazed.

Seven Mission Flood Poems

Farmer's Wife

A fifth sense. An angel, changeling or someone
she kept brushing off, had niggled at her elbow
for the last hour. The light went on. Outside
she found her baby's pram, wheels deep
in swirling water.
The radio announcer
said: *On this island,*
the dike is gone!

Station

The volunteers' tents
at Harrison Mills
all set in the cemetery
Oh! Hurray! Hurray!

The Remains

Rotted shakes, the hole in the roof,
then drop through the rafters,
past the ceiling,
look into the twilight below,
a room's Gyproc paper,
its lime
leached out,
flails about.

See the rows of boneless
figures wave along the walls.

Their ghostly forms
in eerie light, sway and flop.
A ghoul's dance.

After the Flood

The eerieness
of a sofa with
a one-inch beard
of mold, as it
floats around
the floor.

Noah's Ark

Tiers and tiers of baby rabbits
scientifically numbered, crossed,
mated, selected. Crossed again.
Baby rabbits tiered
by the hundreds.

The rescuers found two tiers of them drowned.
Randomly threw the top tiers, still alive
into gunny sacks and released them
on the other bank. Their boat
renamed Noah's Ark.

Over the flooded flats,
punts go back and forth,
rescue a family dog.

A log goes by bucking
the furious river. On it
a cat clings, floats
out of sight
unheard.

Cat's Tongue

Four days after the flood
imagine the house with water
to the man's armpits. A sack of flour
wet on the kitchen counter,
on it a half-starved mother cat
feeding a kitten.
He drilled holes through his house
to let the water out.

The Snake

Water laps at the land
and, there in its long rotting
grasses a snake, its
head above water, slithers forward
body arced, tail down.
It flashes towards shore,
beady eyes on the edge,
its split tongue's
flicker
a witching switch
danger,
danger.

Swan Lake
(the farm in late fall)

Green fields flooded deep on one side
reflect pewter blue
skies draw the eyes.
White swans at Illahae Farm.
As if in rehearsal for southward migration
each sits beside his tan-coloured spouse.
Flocks of snow-white clouds, their long
necks, dark heads etched on the horizon,
a handle to heaven.

Stubs of corn stalks left from the fall
cobs from the fodder pile
bright pink thread-like worms
transform corn to soil.

The swans feed. Gossip, Rise. Their
mellow bugling calls echo
through the valley. Soon
another flock circles the field
lands as a ballet troupe, their
thin white tutus.

A single gunshot pounds the earth
and fear-surged, the flocks' startled
wings clap high into a V, circle
and fly towards Mission.

Two hunters
come out of the duck-blind on the neighbour's farm,
whistle their retriever
to fetch the game.

Trumpeter swans at Illahae Farm
(its "No Hunting" sign), glide
across the pond, its pewter water, unalarmed.
White clouds stretching to heaven,
dark heads pointing upwards, through pungent
gunshot smoke, fields
their misty stage.

Eagles of Illahae Farm at Silver Creek

I

Eagle, you and Silver Creek's
cottonwood tree
consummate marriage
every spring—
a confetti
of fluff bolls and pods
bursting eagle down
blown here and there,
a thick snow
on corn fields,
melting into creek
water, licked by
trout and salmon
fingerlings
carried to the sea.

II

Eagle, your nest
deep inside the
cottonwood,
two eggs, proof
of your design,
beak-crazed by
emerging twins
mouths hinged
open, greedy

beneath
blue sky or rain,
hunger
the aerie
scream.

III

Know, I am
eagle, the third
in every clutch. God
made me too.
I was equally
likely to be eagle
as woman with
wanderlust, *wandernde*
in the blood.

IV

And you two
twins born
high up in long
black branches
pushed
to leap
into gliding flight, elegant
deep wing beats
to ride
the sky.

V.

We sibling raptors
chase the wind
drift along Silver Creek,
climb the sky, scream,
circle, roll
over and over, grip talons in
play.

VI

Soul, you are eagle
veering up,
riding sky.
As I watch,
my stomach-pit flies
and I too, circle
rise and fall,
straddling the wind.
I am your sibling, twin.
Wait for me. I buck your blue
sky, perform my dives
against the wind along the cliffs
plunge saw-toothing, rolling at the
top of each loop. In dreams
I fly as you.

VII

Listen, I hear your
high pitched scream:
krery-krery-krery
tske, tske, tske, and
vivivi, vivivi.
I am
outside, upturned face,
eager to ride with you again,
to fly together,
to chase through wind,
space
and dream.

VIII

An eagle parent
watches. Soars
elegant, hundreds
of feet above, riding up
drafts, long narrow
raked-back wings
glide with drooping
tips, hither and yon
an autumn leaf
remembering
spring.

IX

She dives as
if into sea, but lands
in the arms of the
cottonwood tree.
Calls
to the new clutch.
Lands on
the nest, home
before the leap. Babies screech,
afraid to miss
the birthing branch,
hidden in leaves
too small to return.

X

We circle, shriek and scream
chase the breeze, egg
each other to land. We
soar, call: *yee-yee-yee*
and screech:
krery-krery-krery
but she sits still and tall.
We dive with
an inelegant thud
amidst bouncing talon,
wrapped branch, the
shredded leaf.
Home, the aerie.
Home, Illahae.

Mount Baker — The Nature of Women

You, ancient woman
sit, squatted on a mound
hands on knees, smoke rising
above your head, squinted icy eyes
tormented frown.

You mark a world's inevitable change,
skirts around the hem
of your frosty hill-gown blown in autumn
wind. Tilled fields, warm manure still
rising as it's spread. The nostril flares,
and the stench piles in clouds
against Mission's hills.

You, devil woman, atop the core
see l'aurore "the light of dawn is
before us," watch sunset
on your own inner violence.
Squat Kali, on the ring of fire,
hold down the volcanic lid
on your rhythmic destruction.

You are history and possibility.
Squat, Baker-woman—
rise above the drowning valley's air,
and centuries of people—
Sikh, Mennonite, Hungarian, Indigenous

Pitt Polder Dutch, Latin-American.
Last century's brick factories,
now crowded by malls, suburban
houses, sprawling dairy and fruit farms
all of a piece, the process, a not-history.

Squat woman, watch emergence,
not linear time, watch fluid geography.
This day.

Ancient woman,
this is your dharma, squatted
unalterable, essential,
"This very thing you are."

Still over and over again, we till
the fields, add daily change,
continue to hunt a way in soil
dig for stones, create the day,
a universe, your stance.

The Spider Web, It Glistens

In the morning light, hung with dew
diamonds too heavy for the thread.

Sun rises from behind the mountain
heats Silver Creek's night-cold banks.
Streams of steam rise up eerily.
I tell the children: *Mermaids making tea.*

Along the banks, small trees, beaver dam,
dried blackberry vines, grasses, leaves, corn tassels
all aflash, their pendant diamonds sway, riffled.

Puppy, just out from the house, places a pink foot
gingerly on dew-soaked grass. Tips of kitten tongues
touch ice-cold milk. From his aerie the eagle scans
the creek, silvery half-moon fingerlings
leap at fireflies still ashine in demi-light
on shady banks, skim the creek.

You take my hand, smile and raise my
coat collar around me: *Shall we walk
to the farm house with puppy?*

We step around to miss the spider's web
it glistens. It glistens.

Jed

Every day spring summer fall winter
the crunching cinders beneath your feet
as you paced the lane, each night I listened.

The measured tread belied whatever was going on
in World War II somewhere back of your mind
the now and then of when you walked the town's streets
blankly your eyes meeting mine with no obvious tic or line
of smile. Deeper than the apparent eye
sight, word, sound: *Jed?*
We walked past one another for years
never speaking, but knowing
a silence that ached to burn as sound
to let out the shock of
shells burning ground unbearable noise
and amnesia and God and your dragons
and who knows what
else of your darker days
at war,
that you never talked about, Jed.

Stave Lake Ghazals for the Drowning

I

> *How admirable!*
> *to see lightning and not*
> *think*
> *life is fleeting.*
> —Basho

Deadheads, rooted without roots in putrid brown water.
  They don't
wave as grasses. They are staunch. One end up and one down.

They loom in dark water waiting. Deadheads don't wave, they
lie in wait dark foggy white or pink misty mornings. Teething.

Drowned five loggers! Who were they? Who were they?
Loggers going back to camp from two nights on the town.

A townspeople scurry. It was Hank! And who? And who?
And who? And who else went down? Five men, townsmen,
  with him.

Their boat, who steered the boat, chainsaws, gear? In black
  early-morning
fog haze on Stave Lake. Deadheads. Deadheads wait and wait
  without a wave.

II

We have lingered in the chambers of the sea
By sea-girls wreathed with seaweed red and brown
Till human voices wake us, and we drown.

—T. S. Eliot

The cold mountain water. Ice. The boat, its crack and thud
into that
raised head, feet planted in mud, unrelenting, never floating, eons.

Five men flew for moments, landed wet. Prized chainsaws,
sink and sink.
Metal-toed logging boots, the week's food, and a deck of cards.
Heavy feathers.

A logger afraid of woods. He fled them once. The dark arms
reached out,
and he went back in. O'Hara's horseman rode to that
meeting place.

Drive by Stave Lake, it darkens with deadheads of thought
rising, rising
here and here and there! See those Mission men, the
town remembers.

Forty years or two score and the half of ten. The kisses on
that chimera
of a morning as she turned, not wanting to wake. Still yearning
as they went.

The Old Cade House

The Yard

Orange blossoms, purple plums, greengage trees
stinging nettles, and the snaking green blackberry,
support the trumpets of the mordacious morning
glory. Adamant they wind and cling around
the Cade house on the flats, its pungent walnut
tree, blackening husks of fallen nuts.
Underneath, oat grasses in the mat of other years,
orange blossom shrubs, green leaves in bud, here
and there the fully opened flower swayed, flaunted
her bouquet. Home from the mill, they sat and drank
scents with their own thoughts: santara, santara,
attar and truculent clinging memories.

Orange Blossoms

She went out to the porch to catch a breath
between cleaning this, and cooking that,
the baby and the boy's cries and spats.
She caught its fragrance, stopped,
snapped off a cluster of white flowers. Santara.
Her own self, for one clear, astringent moment.

Santara

My mother sat on the porch steps holding
a single orange in her hand. With her thumb
she opened the fruit, folded the first piece

of skin and watched ripe oils burst
and scent her fingertips. She rubbed the santara
rind, its oils and scents over her forehead, her face.
A small gleam in her day.

Her House

The faded maroon ship-lap sided Cade house—
its raw lathe skeleton showed through where her
boys picked at the scabby break in the walls.
Broken plaster, the grit and dust a gravely
sugar underfoot. Grim-jawed she swept it out
over the stoop and listened to his song. Her boys alarmed
at her anger. That old white man
sitting in his flap-backed long johns
all day long.
She listened to his broken-hearted ode,
calmed.

Lament

My mother heard:
Where's my boy? Where's my boy?
The old English gent's lament from
the stoop of his shack, the edge of Cade house
land, at the mill on the river. Toothless, alone
in his reveries and moans, at the end of a lifetime's
work. No wife. A son—who knows where?
He rued his life aloud, for passing workers
and for her with her sons—he strummed at her
heart with his song: *Where's my boy?*

Winter Yard

Winter brambles, a crisp snap underfoot,
their green prickles turned to nails and claws.
Driven by the east wind, raspy on the walls they grab
at the window frame and glass, scratch
all night long: *let me in*. The leafless trees moan.
She wraps her shawl more tightly around her,
waits for her husband's late night return
or two rings on the party-line phone
nailed to the wall, to say he must stay in town.
She waits to turn out the lights,
lock out the yard.

Brothers

The Fraser is our Ganga.
He stands by the river, beyond the mill
hands in pockets, everyday
without tiring of it. Scans water, sky, the pahari—
Mount Baker—rising from the east horizon.
The bank, wild weeping willow brushing the water
under cottonwood trees, oat grasses.

How can we leave its side, your brother and I?
This river, its mills, log booms, beehive
burners, log hauls and saws, boom boats,
peaveys, boom men, sawyers, sawdust.

Every day begins here for us—morning into night—
before the cacophony of morning,
the sun's shards of light,
meditation, greetings, silence, worship.

Away from India the Fraser is our Ganga
at Haney, Hammond, Matsqui,
Mission, Millside, Port Coquitlam, Pitt Meadows, Port Moody,
New Westminister, Mallardville, Mitchell Island,
Steveston, Lulu Island, Richmond.
Whole lives in these waters. These. Our previous lives
float down, encircle the cosmos
join the waters of desh/pardesh. Again.

We have lived by this river every day
of our lives, Kuldip. Our whole lives,
by this flowing river. Our whole lives
flowing—by this river.

Grandpa's Fruit Basket — The Proper Way to Eat Fruit

Carboujha—Cantaloupe

Round green-gold, flat navel,
its umbilical cord cut, this fruit
is birthed all year round in India. Cut in half
carefully divide in six,
with a slice in your hand, run the knife along,
separate flesh from rind and give each child one
beige oyster on the half shell. Afterbirth of seeds, washed
and saved by the hundreds and strung on fine threads,
will be worn as necklaces for days and days.
We longed for the taste, and the word
carboujha, carboujha,
filled us with flesh and juice. Amazed.
We learned cantaloupe grow in the Okanagan,
small hand-sized, green, rough skinned, sweet. By then Grandpa
had gone. So few, too late to deliver.

Amb—Mango

The heavy breast shape of amb,
a slight smell of turpentine in the bitten skin.
There are three hundred and fifty varieties
of amb, plus the one that got away, the colonization
of paisley. Millions of loquacious patterns of amb.
Gently, his fingers caress it—Grandpa is patient—
until the flesh leaves the core,

the soft, yellow-green-red mottles of unbroken skin.
He made a hole at the pointed end, his soft words
chupela, chupela as he put it to the child's mouth.
Ras—rich gold rivulets down a child's chin,
hands and arms, the softened sweet, amb—breast.

The Purple and Yellow Plums

Imagine it—crave it.
The unfulfilled desire for something rare,
denial of its dailyness in our diet.
Try green plum instead, the core cut out, dried
in the sun. Heaped into mustard oil with added pickle spices,
it turns—a bottle of inedible mold. Try ripe yellow plum,
nowhere near the taste of amb. Peaches too sweet,
pears too grainy.
There is no similarity
in the Western world to amb.
Certainly not in plum.

Anardhana—Pomegranate

Red coarse-skinned, round berries. The open star of its mouth
and gold seed. Opened, it runs blood red
rasas. Each amethyst-shaped crystal
white seed embedded in crimson. Rare in the market,
rare in our homes. There are family stories
of how we shared the honey-combed morsels,
each holding fast to a ruby cluster crown,

tart-sweet, yellow memory. We grabbed
for each red tooth we dropped. Remember
how it stained frocks and hands, the joy of
eating, sharing the blood-red anardhana.

Now, glazed and painted,
in clay, rare blue with wine-red
anardhana on the Moorcroft vase on the mantel.

Angur—Grapes

Goochay of red globe grapes held in his giant hands,
my grandpa peeled each grape, took
out the seeds and plopped the fruits one by one
into a row of open mouths as we stood
in front of his chair.

Now, I teach them to say
no! to whole grapes—you'll choke on them.
Nothing small and round until you're five.

(Once he saw a baby in a café
swallow, choke, turn blue and die
on one red grape.)

I peel their grapes.
I buy them seedless.
I come more than half-way to his sweet caution.

Santara—Orange

Peel tangerines, take each segment
from the rind, cut along the membrane's
edge, turn back the skin to free the unchokeable
flesh. *Santara, santara,* the sound of another childhood word.

Parents hate the way we were indulged
children, our ways unsterilized, too much
attention. Past comprehension—
love, the touch, preparing.

Boy on a Farm

Their iridescent shimmer, the ring-necked
low-headed glide through acres of
seed-headed grasses before haying
followed by two egg-sized feathered fluffs
so whisper-fast you wondered if they were really there.
The whoosh and wing beats of the hen veering
off, luring men and boys on
their mowing machines, away.

All day he sat, mowed round and round,
trimmed inwards,
the field an oval-edged tray.

They scuttled ahead, everywhere. He looked grey:
*Dad they couldn't get away, the pheasants
have no legs anymore, the chicks are headless
now, close to the ground.* He jumped from the tractor,
went home to his mom. After the first day's shock
he became just another man on a farm.

> *his mother said butter is rationed,
> his father replied we'll have to hook up a pulley
> and belt to the old butter churn.*

He saw the dog pull down the prize bull calf
blood steamed red on the crusty snow.
Last winter, the ducks on the undrained field ponds
froze into the ice at night. They set up such a squawk.

He and the hired hand cracked sheets to let them out.
All winter long hundreds of acres of ice ponds
froze around webbed feet until his father said: *No,*
you can't go out there anymore. Soon, spring will come.
The rains came. It was April. He forgot the farm's wildlife
on his way to becoming a farmer.

By the age of ten he had seen the girls climb into the silo,
to tramp down the chopped up vines, pods and squirting peas,
had smelled the souring silage as they came out at day's end.
The silo girl in love with the hired man, the girl
who climbed down the ladder inside the silo crying,
talking of tearing inside, her lipstick rubbed off,
a girlfriend holding onto her: *you shouldn't have given in.*
What's another headless pheasant hen?

After his sister finished chucking the hay from the loft,
she climbed down the ladder and thrust her left arm,
hard, into the hayfork leaning there, tines-up.
Afraid of hurting her, he couldn't free her.
She did it herself.

That fall he turned into a farmer.
He could no longer remember his life before the pheasants
left footless, their chicks missed by the mowing machine
still trying to get under the bloody hen mother
for cover. The bull-calf's gurgling death.
It was wartime,

     his parents said the potatoes have blight.

A plane crash, the debris in a neighbour's field. A pilot died.
Old Mrs. Reynolds walked too far onto the beach. Behind her
the tide came in. He remembers,

> *his father thoughtfully saying,*
> *we'll raise sugar beets for the war effort.*

The runnels of blood from heads of dehorned cows,
the udder of the cow who died when her milk got thick
and clumpy, his white angora rabbit that died of shock
when the dog leapt at her cage. His three-year-old brother lost
in the soupy fog, found hours later happily eating
chop suey, in Lau Yee's shack.

Ten years of age, all day he sat
on the tractor pulling discus and harrow
under the sun, the blue bowl of sky, the cattails
in water-filled ditches, the big monarch butterflies in flight
and the occasional owl swooping low looking for mice.
He called himself a farmer.

He laments what he can't remember, the questions he was
too young to ask. Old things seem small and imaginary yet
he knows they were real. At sixty-two, he can't stop the thoughts:

> *his sister's shoe soles melted in the rain. They were cardboard.*
> *His father cut out some linoleum and lined them again. Saying:*
> *When will this war end? We will leave this farm life behind.*

Recalling Home

It used to seem big,
the house Grandpa bought
in Queensborough: *six hundred dollars,*
fifty down, and his name—the deposit.
I was small. I dreamt I fell down the back
stairs—decorated tops and cut-out hearts on the rails.
Even today I have such fear.

This year I went back to the house—
a shack.
Don't say it's the intervening sixty years.
We had to duck
to miss the cover over the main door.
In the pantry we kept our food—
watermelon b-i-g-and-c-o-l-d-and-r-o-u-n-d.
I wrapped my arms about one, tried to pick it up.
It dropped onto the floor into a thousand pieces.
Before my Father could even be mad,
red pulp, black seeds and green rind covered the floor.

They've changed the front stairs.
They used to go straight up from the street.
A thief once hid behind the hydrangeas.
I saw him—I told no one,
he went right in and hid behind the couch
in the living room. My uncles saw him and chased
him down Wood Street, arms waving, shouting: *Robber, robber.*

In the next room Mama held the baby
on her lap. I asked Mama: *Why*
are your legs black and blue?
She gave me her big-eyed stare,
pinched my arm between her
thumb and forefinger. She pointed:
Your grandpa's sitting right there
in the kitchen next to the oven,
don't you know he will hear!

When the men came into
the living room to talk, if we were noisy and bad,
the men, (my Dad) said to us: *If you speak*
up again I'll cut your throat! Or they said: *Why have we*
kept these girls so long? They're the ones we should drown.
I won't forget that stare.

The memories of the house are real
to a five-year-old. The house though
has seen a transformation.
I won't forget that stare.

Satin — Olive Green, Coral and Cream

Rare satin, heavy olive green, coral and cream
yards and yards of it. For bedspreads, or just to
unfold and look at, and she warned, she
wanted the white sewn for her,
a satin salwar/kameez when she died.

On coral satin Mama embroidered
fans, flower baskets and
peacocks that marched up the middle,
tails splayed in iridescence.
That white woman smocked the sides and
sewed in the cord for our bedspread.
The Punjabi women thought her
a sewing machine wizard.

Rare satin lay in Mama's trunk
waiting a use, seldom moved, but
on occasion, she unfolded it and draped it
just to see it shine and then
folded and put it away again.

Now, its folds are as creased as reused
tissue, the corners worn, a lifetime
of sitting has rounded them off
as with any good life. The white satin used
as she wanted a long time ago, and in the
trunk, rare satin, heavy olive green,
coral and cream, its corners of worn-out holes.
Useless but for these reveries.

Dharma of Punjabi — This and That...

He sat behind the counter
a young man.
He looked like us.

My parents are Indians—from Kenya.
It was a long time ago—they care about those things,

Are you a Punjabi? she asked.

He shrugged.

I was born in Kelowna—so I don't know.

And shrugged again,
pursed his lips and said:

I'm adopted, you know?

Bill Miner's Notebook

Bill Miner's Notes

I'm making a collection, pasting up everything I can find. The evidence, what people said, what they wrote about me. All the legal flim-flam will be included. The Canadian film they call a classic: *The Grey Fox*, courtesy of Mercury Records in Vancouver, is still in the can, but recorded. Posters offering rewards for my capture after the Mission Junction train robbery, and all the notes of our elaborate plans, are here.

You might wonder what I'm doing here. There is a mortality span between here and formerly. You know that formerly, for me, ended. It lies six feet under a concrete slab in Hill Cemetery in Georgia. Miller, Joseph, and Moore donated that "lo que pasa."

I aim to be however, a brilliant ghost. Just behind the curtain. I'm madder than hell that the film left out Mission Junction. I demand—no, I want—Tarantino's attention. Although this notebook's not exactly the caliber of his film *Pulp Fiction*, it has gumption.

If they wish, next time around, (it's karma—I'll be born again), I'll redo the action. I'll make it meaner, leaner, and extend the train robbery section so there's a more accomplished present. If the going gets tough, you can refer Tarantino to Edward Dorn's *Gunslinger*. I loved "I, Horse and Lil." Darn sure got the philosophy right!

He said:

> *Nevertheless,*
> *it is dangerous to be named*
> *and makes you mortal.*

It happened just like that to me—look at these notes, study them and see. Lastly, my agent in life for the rewrite on Mission Junction is Amer Singh.

Bill Miner Explains

We picked Mission Junction for the robbery—
1904—it was a sleepy town in the Fraser Valley.
The night was foggy, the air went through you, cold as
ice water in winter. We had prayed for just this kind of night.
No one was watching outside, so there we were, up the
water tower, holding on for dear life, waiting. Jack Terry,
Shorty Dunn and I knew we could board the train without
getting caught. All we needed was the fog. Inside the
train station the passengers were just like us—impatient,
and on edge, we were all waiting for a train that was
very late.

If we had known then we were Canada's first train robbery
we might have worked harder at setting the gold standard.
        Strum...
           Strum...
              Strum...

Amer Singh — On Bill Miner

Here we sit, eating mangoes
in India amidst our family
as if we had no fears, were safe in Canada
as if we sat there too and savoured the sun
honeyed yellow mangoes dripping
through our fingers, down our chins,
each evening, listening,
heard the bulbul's song,
the cucurooing dove, broke
the many facetted ruby
pomegranates apart, and ate their tangy flesh
picked persimmons, bit through sweet-citrus
lip-puckering skins,
shared with feeding
ants on the ground.

Let me tell you a vaht!
Of what it was to work
in Mission, in Canada, then.

Ah mere vaht!

We heard the transcontinental CPR Engine 440
a dragon shrieking, clawing through the fog
as it nosed into Mission Station
Saturday night, September 10, 1904.
Late, it parted a path. Light reflected a shining circle,

burst through, sounded bell and whistle.
Passengers wrung out with waiting for the train
ran—baggage underarm—or in hand,
to the platform. Brakes ground
to stop exactly at the station door.
Scott shouted: *We're late! All aboard! All aboard!*
Three passengers climbed off as
others got on. He spurred the giant chuffing
dragon to lug its load
along the tracks,
half-blinded with looking, peering through porridge
shoulders tense, rounded forward, eyes peeled for deer,
farmers, cows or coyotes, other denizen on the track
at Mission Junction, at the Silver Creek Bridge, or the dale.

Scott told me he didn't hear the stranger climb aboard until
someone tapped his shoulder, softly
said: *Hands up!*
someone with a soft-brimmed hat—Bill Miner
pushed two Colts (silver-tipped) into Scott's back
towards his heart. He felt ice-cold steel.
Someone polite. A dark cloth mask showed glasses,
red-veined eyes through slit gashes,
wrangler's coarse, cracked grained hands,
sunburned skin, blue-black frock coat
racked on small shoulders, a five-foot-five frame.
Scott saw another revolver too and two hands
holding a rifle.

One. Then, two other robbers. Dacoits,
crowded into CPR Locomotive 440.
They shouted: *Stop at Silverdale Crossing*!

Scott reached, hit the brakes.
They bit and screamed, steel to steel and
the train stopped dead in the haze
ahead of the flats.

One dacoit jumped down
uncoupled the engine, baggage and mail.
Left the passenger cars on the main
international track, unflared,
marked—a target.

Someone climbed up into the engine
said: *Go! Drive on to Whonnock!* A mile past
the church—a bit too far—the engineer
stopped the train, gave two blasts,
almost at Donatelli's farm—angry robbers
fired two shots. Scared the kids staring
from their windows, down onto the train.

Donatellis hid their children
under beds, in cupboards. Turned out lights
to make it dark, to hide.

A robber jumped down from the engine,
came to the baggage and mail car
where I sat. On the sacks. My turban

wound tight around my head against
the mist and cold, I tried to hide a small
safe, gold dust, bonds, currency and bullion.
In the dimly lit night, I sat. Guarding.

When the man banged on the door, shouted:
Open up, let me in!
Express Manager Herbert Mitchell opened the door.
Bill Miner came in, two-colted steel drawn, hands
controlled and strong fingered, knees loosely bent,
under command. Softly, to Mitchell: *Where's
the gold?* Mitchell croaked: *There is none.*
His mouth taut, throat tight, eyes
frightened. He opened the door of the largest safe.
The bandit mused a moment, turned, saw that
I sat on sacks.

A hard smile, he turned from me:
Open it up, he said, softly.
Mitchell opened the vault. Gold dust shone.
The robbers scooped it up, grabbed currency, bonds,
sealed letters. All, stashed in a sack.

I waited, frozen in the black night.
Waited for the shots from the Colt
that would finish Mitchell, slam my heart.
I was ready to pounce at any chance
to take my kirpan, to slash,
behead,
to run.

The robber's eyes snapped at mine.
Quietly, he said: *Hands up!*
The dacoit's eyes met mine. Kindly.
I held my breath. The papers
said he never harmed the crew.

Billy Miner only robbed
the Company.

Ah mere vaht!
Utho paghe raht!

Amer Singh — The Rest of the Story

...Thika dhum, thika dhum,
dhi dhum dhin...

I miss the meaning of my own part
in the play of life
Because I know not the parts
that others play.
—Rabindranath Tagore

They will tell the rest of the vaht
tonight. The parts the others played
in the train robbery at Mission.
They will tell the rest of the vaht
tonight.

I miss the meaning of my own part
in the play of life.

Though I was there, it seems
as if I was not.
They will tell the rest of the vaht
tonight.

Because I know not the parts
that others play.

Nathaniel J. Scott was my boss.
After the robbery
the train went on to Vancouver.
They reported the loss, filed reports,
were interviewed by the RCMP and
met the Pinkerton interrogators.

The robbers escaped.

>   …Thika dhum, thika dhum,
>   dhi dhum dhin…

Amer Singh — At the Donatelli Farm That Night

> ...Thika dhum, thika dhum,
> dhi dhum dhin...

You know our old Punjabi saying:
Yesterday's infants are today's old men?

That was certainly the case then. On that farm
it was the old women who were scared
and shrieking—as if any bandit would try to hide there!

The children ran around shouting
and laughing.

Can you just imagine the din
in that household? The fear...

Listen to their tale...

> ...Thika dhum, thika dhum,
> dhi dhum dhin...

Nathaniel J. Scott, Engineer — The Night of the Robbery

I was appalled.
We never thought Canada's trains might get robbed—
not often at any rate, and not much—though we took
all care and precaution.

Miner never meant to harm me.
After the shock of three bandits
(*On my train! In my engine!*)
I wasn't afraid. Miner said softly:
Do what you are told and not a hair
of your head will be harmed.

I believed him. I had my fellows
and passengers to protect.
I blurted out: *I'm at your service.*
And I went along, started and stopped
when they ordered, at their will.

Shorty Dunn, the other robber,
was another thing. I was leery
when they asked me to go with him,
get out of the engine, take the torch
to bang on Mitchell's car, tell him:
Open up or the car will be blown up.
When he asked: *Who's going to blow it up?*
I said: *These fellows. Here.* Just then a
robber poked a rifle under his nose.

They told him to get down. Grabbed
his gun as he hit the ground
then ordered him back in. Again,
it was Miner who reassured us, saying:
We won't hurt a hair of your heads—
it's your money I want.

Mr. Donatelli

Our older children jumped out of bed and shouted:
The train's stopped at Silverdale Junction!

We heard two toots from the engine.
My wife almost fainted.
Four shots! It wasn't hunting season.
The youngest children hid in cupboards.
A faint fog circled the headlight,
a barely chuffing railway engine.

It stopped.

A barely chuffing railway engine.
A faint fog circled the headlight.
The youngest children hid in cupboards.
Four shots! It wasn't hunting season.
My wife almost fainted.
We heard two toots from the engine.

The train's stopped at Silverdale Junction!
Our older children jumped out of bed and shouted.

Bill Miner — On the $500 REWARD Poster

They got it almost right, but, Christ…
he must have been arresting women to
write I have large wrist-joint bones.
And scars? Hardly noticeable
'cept in summer when my skin goes brown.
They're both on one leg—the right shin
and, Ah! they list the tattooed blue bird
at the base of my right thumb
and my ballet girl—same forearm!
It's Lil, wearin' blue. If only
they knew—when I close my eyes
she dances for me! She dances!
How we two conjoined at the bar.
She touched the moles
they write about, rubbed her pinky
finger soft over each of 'em,
two opinions, that go on and on.
A counterpoint
that dances together, memory and poster
sketched by hand, and mouth.
Her tongue tasting each and every spot
on my "centre breast and under the left breast,"
her pink tongue pirouetted, flicking as if on
pointed toes.

The black and white poster shows me
with uncombed grey hair—shadowy skin.

She wouldn't recognize me.
And who the hell was gonna make me
bare my butt to see that discoloured spot?
After all the real and obvious marks,
was that cheek the crowning star?

Bill Miner — On Maisie

We got away. Left in a hurry
and I ended up in a small town, above Princeton.
A settled man, respected, I worked in a mine.
I played it slow and easy. People there,
like Maisie's folks—they liked me.

That girl Maisie was nice. So lonely.
No one to play with all day long. Summers
are fine for a child, but what could she do in
the long dark days of winter when nights
are long, days short and without sun.

I flooded the low corner of their farm
so she could skate. Skating is solitary, easy to learn.
It makes you feel free. I had it in my mind that
she was so small she'd just float on that pond.
It wasn't hardly any work and I felt good. She even
said:

It'll break the monotony of the long winter days.

God! It's humbling. So little—so much gratitude.
She thinks my name is George Edwards.

Maisie — On Seeing the Bill Miner $500 REWARD Poster

Yes. It's Him! Mr. George Edwards
in the picture. They are wrong!
He never did it. He was my favourite person
in the whole town. Mom and Dad let him
come and help on the farm.
He worked for two whole days, to stop the stream
and flood the field for me so that I
would have a place to skate and play.

Nobody said he had to do it,
he just came and started right in and
never left until it was done. Cut the grass,
the rushes that stuck through and above
the iced-pond. So proud. At the end
he took me out and let me spin, spin, spin!

He was a southern gentleman—told me
he was from Lo Que Pasa Villa.
He lived in Princeton and now and then,
in Nicola Valley.

His name was Mr. George Edwards.
Not William Miner, Robber.
Prisoner No. 10191.

Bill Miner — On Jack Terry

Jack Terry was so thorough that I was never scared. Jack knew
what he was doin'. Jack Terry was the brains that
thought out the Mission Junction one. He planned
it—and sold us on it when we visited Seattle, Shorty
Dunn and me. Dunn was my sidekick and he did
whatever I wanted—no trouble there. Jack Terry
was a loner, always ahead of everyone else, he'd
think everything through while he strummed
his blues guitar.

Jack Terry's Glosa

I met in Mesilla
the cautious gunslinger
of impeccable personal smoothness
and slender leather encased hands
                    —*Gunslinger*, Edward Dorn

Strum...
            Strum...
                        Strum...

I've met them all—Billy the Kid and Billy Miner
barely out of the old lady's string bag. Sixteen!
He robbed the San Francisco stagecoach.
It was his profession, he said, counting his successes,
as if our jobs were guesses—his alone were planned.
We were bored to death with his tales in the Lo Que Pasa Villa.
Still, Bill Miner was a gentleman,
his stories bold, with or without the load,
the most deevine tequila, that ever
I met in Mesilla.

My name is Jack Terry, I can tell you now
Miner was polite—not the brightest mind—he took
no chances, hand picked his fellas, gained
their trust, he convinced them—owned their brains
by buying them everything they wanted.
Most were dumb followers, guitar stringers
high binders, petty thieves, they rode

the rails, hid in brambled hobo jungles.
A gentle heart controlled the 44 Colt's itchy finger—
the cautious gunslinger.

Lady Luck's a bitch. I'd rather trust this crystal ball,
at least it shows me the future. If Billy Miner
was born again in 2007, he'd be hauling in,
driving a Masserati with a bluebird icon matched
to the tattoo at the base of his thumb.
On his right forearm the ballet dancer in process.
He'd be cool as the Yellow Rose of Dawn,
wear mescal buttons on his pleated blouse cuff. Recall,
"Miss Lil reading her encyclopedia," said he had the finesse
of impeccable personal smoothness.

They say I'm cruel and vicious. Not so.
I had the load: *control them; figure out how to get the loot.*
Used my trainsman's training; climb the pole; tap the codes.
Which Express carried the gold? The Mission Junction plan
was based on my knowledge of history from the Rio Grande.
Miner could be sure Shorty Dunn would carry it out.
Dunn dressed like a gold miner. Miner dressed to the hilt
with the Colt, its carved ivory handle,
rings on a wedding finger, two gold and amethyst bands
and slender leather encased hands.

Strum...

Strum...

Strum...Strum!

Bill Miner — On His Horse, Pat

In Princeton, BC, I bought myself a horse exactly
the kind that was to my liking all my life.
She was pure white, intelligent, and stood more than
fifteen hands tall, like a lady Amazon.

My horse Pat was smart. A white steed in the old
fashioned sense of knights, ladies, knaves and
Round Tables. I had this dream where riding
her I floated on the wind. Her long mane and tail
flying like blond hair and her hoofs swimming in the breeze.
That's how she rode—so fluid—long strides—with ease.

I wanted to share that part of Pat with the kids
teach them to ride without spurs. They could
control her with their knees.

For on my horse Pat, it would be
like being on a driver-less horse.
That's how she rode—so fluid—
long strides—with ease.

Bill Miner's Horse Pat — On Bill Miner

Bill thinks I'm part of a carousel, not one horse.
His muse has always been eloquence and poetry.
I've seen worse kids than these—but every Saturday—
it's beginning to wear on my nerves
to say nothing of getting saddle sores. He rounds them up—
all the kids in town and gives them
a ticket to ride around on me. Perverse!
They put their heels into me like spurs—pull my mane, shout
and curse, play good and bad cowpoke, cowboy villain, sheriff.

Bill's idea of a smart horse is to have
me click my hoof to the number he points at
on his gold Omega's face. As if I care about time!
It's space, space, I'm clicking for,
if they only knew—this horse isn't a carousel
of whistles and bells, going round and round played
as if by piano keys. No sir!

At times confusion reigns. I'm not sure Bill
remembers the difference between stagecoach horses
and what he does now—that business
about horsepower and an Iron Horse. Still,
life with Bill is good. He's kind, combs me
for hours with the curry comb until its serrated edges
scratch red ridges in my skin. He does this everyday.
It makes people laugh to watch him groom me,
as if we were going on parade when
it's only for the kids' carousel ride
on Saturday.

Bill Miner — On Kate Flynn

When I think back—I didn't have much education—
I've done alright in teaching myself. There was a
lot of time for that. Thirty-five years in San Quentin.
We had books and papers. That's how I learned
about the East. Tagore and Walt Whitman.

The one thing that I wanted
was to sit and weave, like Mahatma Gandhi.
I dreamed of going to Persia one day, to become
a Pasha, of how I'd look seated on a Tabriz,
with a ornamented turban. It always
seemed right to me.

Men there have a certain freedom to be with their men
friends and, as Mahfouz writes, to be with
their women.

Kate Flynn knew more about me than anyone.
If I was to relive that part,
I'd listen to more classical music with Kate,
and learn about photography, her art. And now,
to be honest, I pine for a purer heart,
and to be with Kate Flynn.

Bill Miner's Ghost — On Weaving a Persian Carpet

I first saw the rug in Lil's saloon
as we lay on it, in the half-dark. I couldn't tell
where it began, and Lil's skin ended. So smooth
that when I ran my hand against the pile I wondered
if it was wool or the milk-smooth silk that covered her.
She traced her fingers over the pattern and told stories.
As if we were living the Arabian nights
and she was the first Scheherazade.

Twenty-five years in Lo Que Pasa Villa,
there was time to wonder about the woman
who spun the yarns, dyed the wool and
the man who strung the double-loom
with warp and weft, tied the knots according
to the patterns flowing through Persian blood.

By candlelight the colours gleamed. Royal reds,
blues, greens, creamy whites. The tapestry with a tree,
its branches laden, ripe. At each end a white kilim
and a hand-twisted fringe. I couldn't stop
thinking this was more than just a rug.
This was a chronicle, a record, a knotted story.

I've got an idea! I'll change the way I lived before
and loom and reweave my life,
like nomads who weave dream gardens
of water, and brilliant flowers

into bags, tent flaps and Persian carpets
as they sit in the middle of dunes and sand.
I'll sit like them at the loom in front
of the unravelling rug. I'll keep the warp
that makes the upright strings and weave
the weft again—change the colours and
patterns of my former life.
I'll decide what to add—where to darken,
the colours of what I threw away. The pattern
will include the turbaned Sikh
who crouched on the safe at Mission Junction.

And how shall I weave it? As Amer Singh said:
You can't change all your past. It was your kismet.
You improved your karma—never hurt a soul.
Now move on through the cycles,
to your own next good birth.

I'll weave the weft with Kashmiri pashmina
wool, in creamy French white to show the fog
at Mission Junction. I'll knot my ballet dancer
with the silk yarns of Isfahan sky, clad against
indigo blue. Use Kurdish green and khaki gold for
the kind men at Lo Que Pasa Villa.
Weave dughi rose for Maisie as she
skates across the Nicola Valley pond.

I'll plait the rest in, strong but mellow, gentle
as the breeze that riffled Kate Flynn's auburn hair.
I'll use black dye—made from acorn cups

and oak galls—to draw the piano. I remember
how wind carried the notes and scores
of Kate's music. It spiraled over the hills
spinning from the wax cylinder rolls, wafted under
trees, meandered along august hills coloured
madder orange and umber. Through the brown
scrub pine, spruce, peeling birch, it skimmed
and rustled the dry grasses, then puffed and rolled
the balls of sagebrush against one another, into one.

I will compose it myself—a symphony!
And organize it like a sonnet. For Kate.

I'll weave the wind in indigo bands,
the clouds in drifts of white spun
silk yarn. Gentle elephants rolling across
the sky. A heavenly gateway.

I'll use the combs to press down each weft string.
Beat knots into place to make the pile. This
life I weave will go with the ebb and flow
of the whole. I'll pay attention to making knots,
use the colours as the Master Weaver calls:
red, not blue; blue not yellow; yellow not green;
green not madder brown, as he rolls them out for me,
this weave that makes a life—not the jarring colours
I put into my last life.

The new pattern will be rhythmical, I'll border it
in feathery leaves—weave in palmettes, knotted

roses and tracery. It will speak with the local
accents: Princeton, Mission, Hope, Kamloops,
and Nicola Valley. Written out by hand, it will
shine. A talim for the next generations.
I will weave forever with my fellow man,
no more against the grain.

Bill Miner — On Kate Flynn (Again)

She could be fierce and independent;
she left Chicago to live on the frontier.
She wanted to be a photographer. It wasn't what women
did then. She wanted to record how life—to some—was
cruel. She was creating a local archive.

We met in Kamloops. Kate had a small studio there,
she divided it in half with a woven tapestry and lived
in the room behind it. We two would eat
dinners she cooked, drink wine and listen
to her classical music.

Kate told me the Pinkerton detective was on my trail,
working with the RCMP. She said I had to leave
soon, agreed to go back to Chicago where
I was to meet her. I promised we would go
on a trip to Europe.

Kate Flynn — On Bill Miner

Here I am on this damn train on my way back to Chicago
with all the cameras packed, films, glass plates, tripods, lenses
everything in crates. Back to a place I'd left and didn't
expect to go to again. Alone. It's hard to believe I have
agreed to this.

As the train wheels hum and clack, they seem to be saying:
Bill will come. Bill will come.
Or is it just my mind reeling, trying to take in the last
unbelievable year? Wishing?

We met when I took the pictures for Constable Fernie
of the family killed near Chilcotin Crossing.
I focused the lens and clicked the shutter
fast, half-closed my eyes not to see.
Bill bolstered my courage. We left there, together,
Bill and me.

He loves my music—looks at my pictures—sees
everything, as if we have one set of eyes.
We take pictures just for fun,
then Bill tells me what I tried to capture in each
particular one. Even when I focus on the smallest
detail to puzzle him, he knows what I have done.

How will I stand to be away from him? So gentle.
His eyes look down rather than see me frown. In those

first blue and sunny days he picked wild daisies,
mixed with blue bachelor buttons as
blankets to cover me as I lay bathing in the sun.

Is the Bill I know, the whole?
There's a patina of age and use, a little tarnish.
Do I know the man I love? For whom I give up all
I ever worked for, to go back to Chicago—a town
I loathe—but that is our best hope?

He will come, I know. He's never let me down.
Bill says the daisy petals prove his love.
He loves me—he loves me not—he loves me!

Amer Singh — The End

...Thika dhum, thika dhum,
dhi, dhum dhin...

The last I knew of Bill Miner and Kate Flynn
was a story—years later—in a
newspaper from Los Angeles
that said a woman named Kate Flynn
went to Europe. She stayed there for several
years, accompanied by a mining engineer.

They were interested in photographic arts.
They were making a collection of Persian carpets.

Ah mere vaht...
Utho paghe raht.

...Thika dhum, thika dhum,
dhi, dhum dhin!

Notes

The following are the poems that have been published in journals: "Letter to Peter Trower—Sechelt Penninsula, BC" appeared in *BC Studies*; "The Clicks and Snaps of a School Day" appreared in *CV2;* "Seventeen—Summer Job at Aylmer's Cannery" appeared in *Event;* "The Old Cade House" appeared in *Event*. Earlier versions of "Bill Miner's Ghost—Weaving a Persian Carpet" and "Amer Singh—The End" appeared in *WordWorks* Summer 2009. Earlier versions of "Bill Miner's Ghost: Weaving a Persian Carpet," "Letter to Peter Trower, Sechelt Peninsula, BC," "The Mills of Mission—Embers and Sparks," "The Mill Where the Men in My Family Worked (1920s)," "Mill Kids—After School," "The Stream at the Bottom of the Gulley," "Alpha Towns—The Valley's North Shore" appeared in *Event* 38/2 (Fall 2009).

In this book, I use the concept of *lieu de mémoire*, that is ideas about places, the sites, and the realms of history, to talk about the memorial heritage of my family and people during a particular time. The sites of memory are important as they take into account the regions or places that have made up my life (Punjab, India, and our villages there), Queensborough, Mission, East Delta, Ladner, the Fraser Valley, British Columbia and Canada.

I think of memory as life rather than as history. Memory is made up of remembering and of forgetting, and is subject to appropriation and manipulation. Sometimes, along the way, we also change what we remember: we generate new meanings in the light of present day understanding and we often resurrect old meanings. During this process we may establish unforeseen connections that might not have been predictable earlier. That is the beauty of the concept of *lieu de mémoire*, which I discovered while at the Leighton Colony at Banff. It appears in Zeynep Çelik's "Colonial/Postcolonial Intersections: lieux de mémoire in Algiers," *Third Text 49*, Winter 1999–2000. For those interested in this concept, Çelik is developing the ideas of Pierre Nora, *Between Memory and History: Rethinking the French Past*.

I have used the concept in many ways. Memory, myth and my imaginative embroideries and appropriations are in this sutra (historical text).

In the poem "Mount Baker—The Nature of Women," I have used found words from Sherman Paul in *Olson's Push: Origin, Black Mountain and Recent American Poetry*, (Louisiana State University Press). He credits Mao Tse Tung with the line, "the light of dawn is before us." Poet Charles Olson used this and other fragments from one of Mao's speeches in his poem, "The Kingfishers." Similarly, I use fragments such as the line, "this very thing you are," from Olson's poem.

The quoted lines in "Ghazal II" of "Stave Lake Ghazals for the Drowning," are the last three lines from T. S. Eliot's, "The Love Song of J. Alfred Prufrock."

In the section "Bill Miner's Notebook," I treat Bill Miner as a Zen cowboy ghost. The "Notebook" is to be read sequentially. It is based on the book, *Bill Miner Stagecoach & Train Robber*, (Heritage House), and on *The Grey Fox: The True Story of Bill Miner—Last of the Old-Time Bandits*, by Mark Dugan and John Boessenecker, (University of Oklahoma Press). I have liberally added fictional characters, events and places.

Throughout "Bill Miner's Notebook," I use the words "lo que pasa." Bill Miner referred to San Quentin prison, where he was incarcerated for over twenty-five years, as "lo que pasa." Here, I also use it to refer to his grave.

The three lines in "Bill Miner's Notes," and for the epigram for "Jack Terry's Glosa," are from Edward Dorn's *Gunslinger*, (Duke University Press). In the latter poem, I have used a number of found words from an earlier edition of Dorn's book *Gunslinger* (Wingbow Press).

In my Punjabi Sikh culture, storytelling in the evening is a very intimate, though formalized event. The words "Ah mere vaht, utho paghi rathe," (That is my story, night has fallen over it), used in the last poem "Amer Singh—The End," are the words each storyteller recites at the end of his or her story. These words signal the end, but also encourage the next storyteller to begin to tell another story, such as in the poem "Amer Singh—Thoughts on Bill Miner."

Kuldip Gill was born in Faridkot District, Punjab, India. She immigrated to Canada at age five and then attended school in the Fraser Valley. She worked in the forestry and mining industries for twenty years and then obtained her PhD in anthropology from UBC. She taught at UBC, SFU, and at the Open Learning Agency, and she taught a creative writing class at the University College of the Fraser Valley. Her poetry has aired on radio and has appeared in *Event, BC Studies, CV2,* and *AMSSA–Cultures West.* She served on the editorial board of *Prism International.* Gill's first book of poetry, *Dharma Rasa* (Nightwood Editions), was a winner of a BC 2000 Book Award. *Valley Sutra* is her final tribute to her two beloved homelands.

Note from the publisher:

Kuldip passed away in May 2009, just one month after she agreed to publish *Valley Sutra* with Caitlin Press. I would like to thank Marisa Alps and Kate Braid for their sensitive and dedicated assistance with the post-humous edit of this manuscript. It is our sincerest desire to publish *Valley Sutra* with the integrity due to Kuldip's work. I would also like to thank Jim McIntosh for his continued faith in Caitlin Press. At Jim's request all royalties from *Valley Sutra* will be donated to support literacy in BC.

—Vici Johnstone